TARANTULAS

by Jaclyn Jaycox

Raintree is an imprint of Capstone Global Library Limited, a company incorporated in England and Wales having its registered office at 264 Banbury Road, Oxford, OX2 7DY – Registered company number: 6695582

www.raintree.co.uk
myorders@raintree.co.uk

Edited by Mandy Robbins
Designed by Dina Her
Original illustrations © Capstone Global Library Limited 2021
Picture research by Morgan Walters
Production by Tori Abraham
Originated by Capstone Global Library Ltd

978 1 4747 9493 0 (hardback)
978 1 4747 9622 4 (paperback)

British Library Cataloguing In Publication Data
A full catalogue record for this book is available from the British Library.

Acknowledgements
We would like to thank the following for permission to reproduce photographs: Alamy: BIOSPHOTO, 22; Newscom: Andrea & Antonella Ferrari/NHPA/Photoshot, 27; Science Source: Kenneth M. Highfill, 23; Shutterstock: Allmy, 12, asawinimages, 17, bchyla, 7, Cathy Keifer, 21, 24, Dan Olsen, 11, Milan Zygmunt, Cover, 18, Nenad Nedomacki, 16, R McPherson, 26, Ryan M. Bolton, 14, Safwan Abd Rahman, 19, socool23, 5, Vaclav Sebek, 1, wawritto, 9, wolfness72, 13, xtotha, 8, 15

Every effort has been made to contact copyright holders of material reproduced in this book. Any omissions will be rectified in subsequent printings if notice is given to the publisher.

Printed and bound in India.

Contents

Words in **bold** are in the glossary.

Amazing tarantulas

Many people are afraid of spiders, especially big, hairy ones! Tarantulas are not a danger to people. They are calm animals. They won't attack unless threatened. Some people even keep them as pets.

Tarantulas are a type of **arachnid**. There are about 900 types. They are the biggest spiders in the world.

Where tarantulas live

Tarantulas live on every **continent** except Antarctica. Most live in South America. They also live in the United States, Mexico, Australia, southern Asia and Africa.

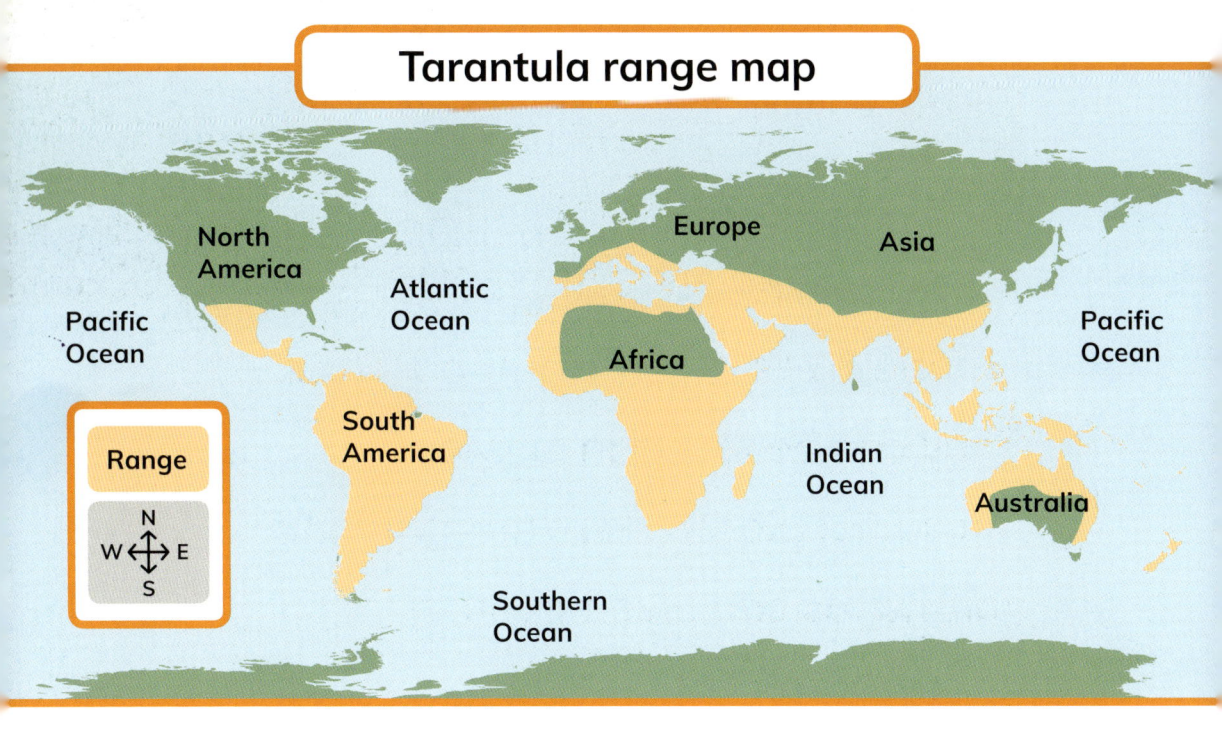

Tarantula range map

North America

Europe

Asia

Atlantic Ocean

Pacific Ocean

Africa

Pacific Ocean

South America

Indian Ocean

Range

Australia

N
W E
S

Southern Ocean

Tarantulas live in warm **habitats**.
They can be found in jungles.
These hot places have many plants.
Tarantulas can also be found in
dry deserts.

Tarantulas live in different places. Most live in **burrows** underground. They dig these holes with their fangs and legs. They put silk on the walls. This stops soil from falling in. They can climb in and out of the hole.

Other types of tarantulas live under rocks. Some live under logs. Some even live high up in trees.

Big, hairy spiders

Tarantulas come in different sizes. Some have legs that stretch across 12.7 centimetres (5 inches). Others stretch across 28 centimetres (11 inches). The smallest tarantulas weigh about 25.5 grams (0.9 ounces). The biggest can weigh more than 99 grams (3.5 ounces).

Tarantulas are different colours too. Many are brown or black. Some are blue or pink. They can also have stripes or spots.

Tarantulas have eight legs. They have eight eyes. Their hair makes them different from other spiders. It covers their bodies and legs. The hair helps them to climb.

The hair also protects them from **predators**. These animals hunt spiders. A tarantula is ready if an animal attacks. It can flick hairs at the attacker. The hair can hurt the attacker's eyes. It gives the spider time to escape.

On the menu

A tarantula waits in its burrow. It's dark outside. It knows an insect is walking past. The tarantula jumps on the insect and bites it. It holds on to the insect until it dies. Then it eats it.

Other spiders use webs to catch food. Tarantulas don't use webs. But some leave a line of silk outside their burrows. When **prey** touches it, the tarantula knows food is there.

Tarantulas hunt at night. They can't see well, but they sense small back-and-forth movements. They sense these **vibrations** with their legs. They can also use their hairs. This helps tarantulas know if something is close.

Tarantulas have strong jaws. When they bite their prey, their fangs let out **venom**. The venom kills their prey. Tarantulas can't eat solid food. They have to turn their prey into liquid. Tarantulas use their straw-like mouths to suck up the animals.

fangs

Tarantulas eat many types of animals. Most tarantulas eat insects. They also eat other spiders and small lizards. They eat mice, snakes and frogs too. Some tarantulas even eat birds. Tarantulas can go for days without food. They often have big meals. They can go for a month between meals.

Tarantulas also drink water. They find drops of water on leaves or in puddles on the ground.

Life of a tarantula

Tarantulas spend most of their time at home. They live alone. They only get together to **mate**. A male leaves his burrow to find a female. He builds a web. He dances to attract the females. The males leave after mating. They can't stay too long because the females might try to eat them!

A female lays between 50 and 2,000 eggs. She wraps them in silk. This keeps them safe. After six to nine weeks, the eggs hatch.

Baby tarantulas are called spiderlings. Newborns are less than 5 millimetres (0.2 inches) wide. That is half the size of a pea! After hatching, they leave the burrow to live on their own.

old skin

tarantula after moulting

Tarantulas have to **moult** in order to grow. They wriggle out of their old skin. They leave the old skin behind. Young spiderlings moult about once a month. Tarantulas moult until they are 7 or 8 years old.

Tarantulas don't only moult to grow. If they lose a leg, it will regrow while moulting.

Males can live for up to 7 years. Most die not long after mating. Female tarantulas live longer than males. They can live for up to 30 years in the wild.

Dangers to tarantulas

Few animals eat tarantulas in the wild. Birds, large lizards and snakes sometimes eat them.

Tarantula hawks are the biggest danger. These are large wasps. They sting tarantulas. Then they lay their eggs on the spiders. When the eggs hatch, the young wasps eat the tarantulas.

Habitat loss is a danger to some tarantulas. When trees are cut down the tarantulas that live there lose their homes. People also keep tarantulas as pets. But too many are being taken out of the wild to be kept as pets. Some types of tarantulas are in danger. They are at risk of dying out. Laws are put into place to protect them.

Fast facts

Name: tarantula

Habitat: deserts, jungles, rainforests

Where in the world: found on every continent except Antarctica

Food: insects, spiders, mice, toads, snakes, small lizards, birds

Predators: tarantula hawks, birds, large snakes and lizards

Life span: males: 5–7 years; females: up to 30 years

Glossary

arachnid group of animals that includes spiders, scorpions, mites and ticks

burrow hole or tunnel used as a home

continent one of Earth's seven large land masses

habitat natural place and conditions in which a plant or animal lives

mate join with another to produce young

moult shed an outer layer of skin

predator animal that hunts other animals for food

prey animal hunted by another animal for food

silk thin but strong thread made by spiders

venom poisonous liquid produced by some animals

vibration fast movement back and forth

Find out more

Books

Bugs (DK findout!), DK (DK Children, 2017)

Scorpion vs Tarantula (Animal Rivals),
Isabel Thomas (Raintree, 2017)

Tarantula vs Tarantula Hawk: Clash of the Giants
(Minibeast Wars), Lindsy O'Brien (Raintree, 2016)

Websites

www.bbc.co.uk/cbbc/watch/bp-meet-charlotte-the-tarantula
Watch this video about a redknee tarantula called
Charlotte!

www.dkfindout.com/uk/animals-and-nature/arachnids/goliath-tarantula
Find out about the goliath tarantula.

Index